Famous People

CLEOPATRA

c70~30BC

Christine Moorcroft

Magnus Magnusson

Christine Moorcroft is an educational consultant and an Ofsted inspector, who was a teacher in primary and special schools and a lecturer in education. She has written and edited several books on history and religion and on other subjects, including personal and social education, science and English.

Magnus Magnusson KBE, has written several books on history and archaeology, and translated many Icelandic sagas and modern Icelandic novels. He has presented major television programmes on history and archaeology, such as *Chronicle*, *The Archaeology of the Bible Lands* and *Living Legends*, as well as the long-running quiz series, *Mastermind*. He is currently chairman of Scottish Natural Heritage, the Government body which advises on environmental issues.

ACKNOWLEDGEMENTS

The authors thank the staff of Childwall Library, Liverpool for their help.

Picture credits
Ancient Art & Architecture: pages 10 (necklace), 11 (top), 12, 13 (both coins), 15, 16 (both), 17 (both)
Michael Holford: pages 4, 5, 8, 10 (portrait), 11 (bottom)
AKG: pages 6, 19
Werner Forman: page 18

Published by Channel Four Learning Limited
Castle House
75–76 Wells Street
London W1P 3RE

Written by Christine Moorcroft and Magnus Magnusson
Illustrated by Jane Bottomley
Cover illustration by Jeffrey Burn
Designed by Blade Communications
Edited by Margot O'Keeffe
Printed by Alden Press
ISBN 1-8621-5354-X

For further information about Channel 4 Schools and details of published materials, contact
Channel 4 Schools
PO Box 100
Warwick CV34 6TZ
Tel: 01926 436444
Fax: 01926 436446

Contents

Cleopatra and her family

Cleopatra was a Greek but she was born about 70BC in Alexandria, which was the capital of Egypt at that time. Nearly 300 years earlier, Alexander the Great had conquered Egypt and built the city of Alexandria. Alexander had made Ptolemy I, Cleopatra's ancestor, the Pharaoh of Egypt.

After this, the family called their sons Ptolemy and their daughters Cleopatra, Berenice or Arsinoë.

Alexander the Great, who built Alexandria and named it after himself.

Julius Caesar

Cleopatra

Mark Antony

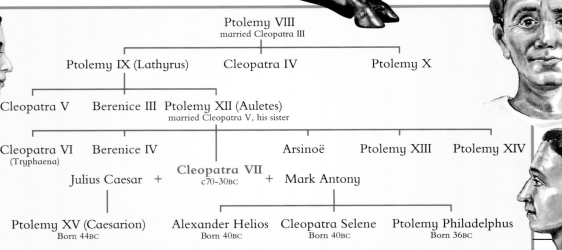

Ptolemy VIII
married Cleopatra III

Ptolemy IX (Lathyrus)   Cleopatra IV   Ptolemy X

Cleopatra V   Berenice III   Ptolemy XII (Auletes)
married Cleopatra V, his sister

Cleopatra VI   Berenice IV   Arsinoë   Ptolemy XIII   Ptolemy XIV
(Tryphaena)

Julius Caesar +   Cleopatra VII   + Mark Antony
c70–30BC

Ptolemy XV (Caesarion)   Alexander Helios   Cleopatra Selene   Ptolemy Philadelphus
Born 44BC   Born 40BC   Born 40BC   Born 36BC

A marble head of Cleopatra which was made in her lifetime.

Cleopatra's father was the Pharaoh of Egypt. Her mother and father were brother and sister. It was the custom for royal brothers and sisters to marry so that they could rule together.

Cleopatra had two older sisters, called Cleopatra Tryphaena and Berenice. Just after Cleopatra was born, her father married again. We do not know the name of his second wife, nor do we know what happened to Cleopatra's mother.

Cleopatra had a younger half-sister, Arsinoë, and two younger half-brothers, both called Ptolemy. They all spoke Greek, even though they lived in Egypt.

ΚΛΕΟΠΑΤΡΑ

This is the name Cleopatra in Greek writing.

This is the name Cleopatra in Egyptian hieroglyphic writing.

Did you know?

- *Egypt had been ruled by Egyptian Pharaohs for 3,000 years before Alexander the Great conquered it in 331BC. Then it was ruled by Greek Pharaohs.*

- *In those days, Cairo, the capital of Egypt today, was just a small settlement without a name.*

5

Growing up in Alexandria

Alexandria was a magnificent city on the coast of the Mediterranean Sea. It had many fine buildings, including royal palaces and marble temples.

There was a lighthouse called the Pharos which was called one of the Seven Wonders of the Ancient World. Built on an island, linked to the city by a causeway, it was a white marble tower 130 metres high. A great fire burned at the top of it to warn sailors about the rocks.

Above: This is an artist's drawing of the Pharos (lighthouse) at Alexandria.

Right: A map of the lands around the Mediterranean Sea.

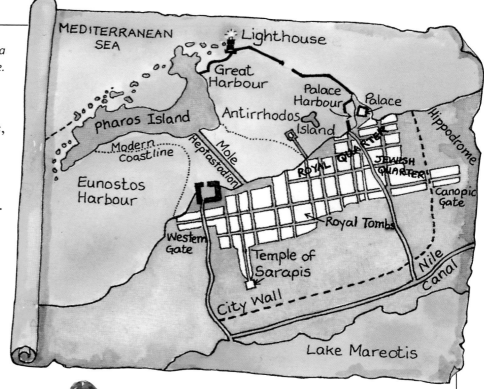

A map of Alexandria in Cleopatra's time.

Cleopatra was taught Greek literature, science, mathematics, astronomy, music and medicine. She also learned public speaking. She was good at all of these and could speak many languages. She enjoyed drawing, singing, playing a lyre and horse-riding.

There were schools in many Egyptian cities for the children of the rich Greeks. They wanted Greek children to be well-educated so that they could rule the Egyptians.

A terracotta figurine, from Cleopatra's Egypt, of a child writing.

Did you know?

- *Alexandria was a great centre of learning. It had the world's largest library.*

- *The land where the royal palaces in Alexandria used to be is now under water.*

- *The Pharos was still standing until the 14th century, when it was damaged by an earthquake.*

7

Cleopatra, Pharaoh of Egypt

Cleopatra's father, Auletes, spent a lot of money while he was Pharaoh. He gave money and expensive gifts to the men who ruled the Roman Empire. To get this money, he made the people of Alexandria pay high taxes. In 57BC the people rebelled and Auletes fled to Rome.

A statue of a Roman soldier.

Cleopatra's eldest sister was made the ruler of Egypt, but she died soon after. So Berenice, her other sister, was made the ruler.

All this time, Auletes was plotting to return to Alexandria and claim his throne. He paid a Roman general to march on Alexandria with a large army. The Romans won the battle. Auletes took over Alexandria and had his daughter Berenice executed.

The Romans fought the people of Alexandria to make Auletes the ruler again.

The Romans went back to Rome but Auletes kept some soldiers to protect him. He made a will which said that Cleopatra and the older of her brothers were to rule together when he died. This meant that they had to marry.

Auletes died in 52BC. Cleopatra, who was 18, became ruler of Egypt with her brother.

Cleopatra and her brother, who was only ten years old, became the Pharaohs of Egypt.

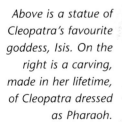

Above is a statue of Cleopatra's favourite goddess, Isis. On the right is a carving, made in her lifetime, of Cleopatra dressed as Pharaoh.

Did you know?

• *When Cleopatra became Pharaoh, Egypt had many problems. The country owed a lot of money to Rome and then there were severe famines. The people were angry about the way the country had been run.*

• *Cleopatra found clever ways to help Egyptian exports of grain, papyrus, linen and vegetable oils.*

9

Beauty, fashion and perfume

Cleopatra dressed in the Greek style, in a long loose tunic. Women in Alexandria wore rich purple robes and, for special occasions, white silk robes and a lot of gold jewellery.

Cleopatra had two women servants, Iras and Charmion, who looked after her clothes, hair and make-up.

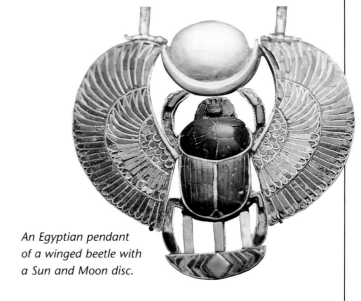

An Egyptian pendant of a winged beetle with a Sun and Moon disc.

This is a Roman portrait of a young woman wearing jewellery.

Cleopatra used make-up to look beautiful and to protect her skin from the sun. Green eye-shadow was made from a mineral called malachite. Kohl, another mineral, was used as an eye-liner. Lipstick was made from ochre, and the plant henna was used to stain nails.

Perfume had been used by the Egyptians for about 3,000 years. Both men and women used to bathe in perfumed oils and rub them into their skin. They also used perfumes when they prayed. Some of the perfumes used were frankincense, myrrh and ben oil.

An Egyptian carving of women making perfume from lilies.

During banquets, servants would scatter flower petals and light incense. Sometimes the women wore on their heads cones of perfumed fat which would melt and the perfumed oil would trickle through their hair and down their bodies.

Above is a wall painting from an Egyptian tomb of women at a banquet, wearing wax head cones and sniffing blue lotus flowers.

Did you know?

- **Egyptian temples had laboratories where perfumes were made.**

- **The recipes for perfumes were kept secret. It was said that perfume was the sweat of the gods.**

The threat from Rome

In 49BC a Roman general named Julius Caesar drove Pompey, the ruler of Rome, out of the city. Caesar was now the ruler of Rome. Pompey had helped Cleopatra's father, so now she helped him. She gave him soldiers and weapons so that he could fight Caesar.

This made everyone in Alexandria very angry with Cleopatra, including her brother and sister, who wanted to get rid of her. So in 48BC she had to flee from Alexandria. This meant her brother Ptolemy, who was only 13, was in charge. He had advisers to help him.

Above is an 18th century picture of the war between Pompey and Julius Caesar.

12

Coins from the Roman Empire showing portraits of Julius Caesar and Pompey.

Then Caesar defeated Pompey's army in Greece, so Pompey went to Egypt for more help. But Ptolemy would not help him in case Caesar invaded Egypt. So Ptolemy killed Pompey.

When Caesar landed at Alexandria, Pompey's head was brought to him by Ptolemy's advisers.

Ptolemy's advisers carried Pompey's head to Caesar.

Did you know?

- **Caesar wanted to be the Roman Emperor. He wanted to defeat Pompey's army but not to harm Pompey. He was sad when he found out that the Alexandrians had killed him.**

13

Cleopatra and Julius Caesar

Caesar went to live in the royal palace at Alexandria as the Roman consul. He sent for Cleopatra and her brother, Ptolemy.

Ptolemy came at once. But Cleopatra was worried that her brother's troops would capture her. She made her journey in secret. She sailed in a merchant ship and, just off Alexandria, climbed into a small boat which took her to the harbour.

A merchant arrived at the palace carrying a rolled-up carpet. He unrolled the carpet and Caesar was astonished to see a young woman jump out of it! It was Cleopatra!

Caesar thought Cleopatra was brave and clever. He fell in love with her.

An ancient Egyptian wall carving of Cleopatra as the goddess Isis and her son, Caesarion, as the god Horus.

Ptolemy was very angry. He wanted to get rid of Cleopatra and Caesar. He had more soldiers but Caesar and Cleopatra managed to keep him out of the palace and take him as a hostage.

Ptolemy's soldiers trapped Caesar's boats in the harbour. So Caesar had all the boats in the harbour set on fire. After a siege of many months, Ptolemy was defeated.

Cleopatra and Caesar had a son, Caesarion. Cleopatra took him to Rome live in one of Caesar's villas.

People in Rome thought Caesar was going to get rid of the Senate and rule alone. On 15th March 44BC a group of them murdered Caesar.

Caesar was murdered by a group of Romans from the Senate.

Did you know?

- **Ptolemy XIII tried to escape from Alexandria by boat, but he was wearing so much golden armour that he drowned.**

- **Arsinoë was taken to Rome as a prisoner.**

- **In 47BC Cleopatra married her younger half-brother, 12-year-old Ptolemy XIV, so that he could rule with her.**

Cleopatra and Mark Antony

After Caesar's death, Cleopatra went back to Alexandria with her son, Caesarion, who now ruled with her.

In Rome there were three new rulers, Octavian, Mark Antony and Lepidus.

Mark Antony set off to conquer more lands for Rome. He went to Turkey. There he sent for Cleopatra, to see what help she could give him.

A marble head of Mark Antony made in his lifetime.

Cleopatra wanted to make a big impression on Mark Antony. She sailed up the river in a barge with a golden deck, purple sails and silver oars.

In Egypt, coins were minted which had Cleopatra's head on one side and Mark Antony's on the other.

Mark Antony's first sight of Cleopatra was of a young woman dressed in a fine silk robe. She was lying on a couch under a golden canopy. Mark Antony stayed with her on her boat for a banquet which lasted for four days! They fell in love.

Mark Antony went to live at the royal palace. Cleopatra promised that her armies would help him.

In 40BC, Cleopatra had twins – Cleopatra Selene and Alexander Helios. Their father was Mark Antony.

Did you know?

- **The Roman Empire was divided between the three rulers, so that Octavian ruled the West, Mark Antony ruled the East, and Lepidus ruled Africa.**

Defeat and death

Mark Antony was still trying to conquer other lands but he lost many battles. Cleopatra's army helped him to conquer Armenia and this time he was a hero.

But in Rome people were angry because Mark Antony had given lands to Cleopatra which belonged to Rome, and he lived with her and not in Rome.

In 31BC, Octavian defeated Antony in a sea battle at Actium. Mark Antony and Cleopatra went back to Alexandria. They knew that Octavian would soon invade Egypt.

A Roman coin celebrating the capture of Egypt.

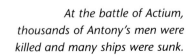

At the battle of Actium, thousands of Antony's men were killed and many ships were sunk.

In July 30BC, Octavian's armies marched towards Egypt. Soon they were at Alexandria. After a long battle, Mark Antony was defeated.

Cleopatra had shut herself up in her tomb with her servants and all her treasures. Mark Antony came back from the fighting and thought she had killed herself. He stabbed himself with a sword. As he was dying, he was told that she was still alive. Servants lifted him into Cleopatra's tomb, where he died in her arms.

Cleopatra knew that Octavian would take her to Rome as a prisoner. So she, too, killed herself. She was buried with Mark Antony.

A statue of Octavian, who defeated Mark Antony.

The death of Cleopatra.

Did you know?

- *The Pharaohs always had their tombs built long before they died. They were buried with their most precious treasures.*

- *The tomb of Antony and Cleopatra has never been found.*

- *Caesarion was murdered. Mark Antony's wife, Octavia, looked after Antony and Cleopatra's children.*

Time-lines

Cleopatra became
Pharaoh of Egypt
with her
brother–husband,
Ptolemy XIII

c70BC

c51

Cleopatra
was born

c70
**Cleopatra was
born**

55
Julius Caesar
invaded Britain

c30
Jesus was
crucified

c570
Muhammad
was born

500BC

0

AD500

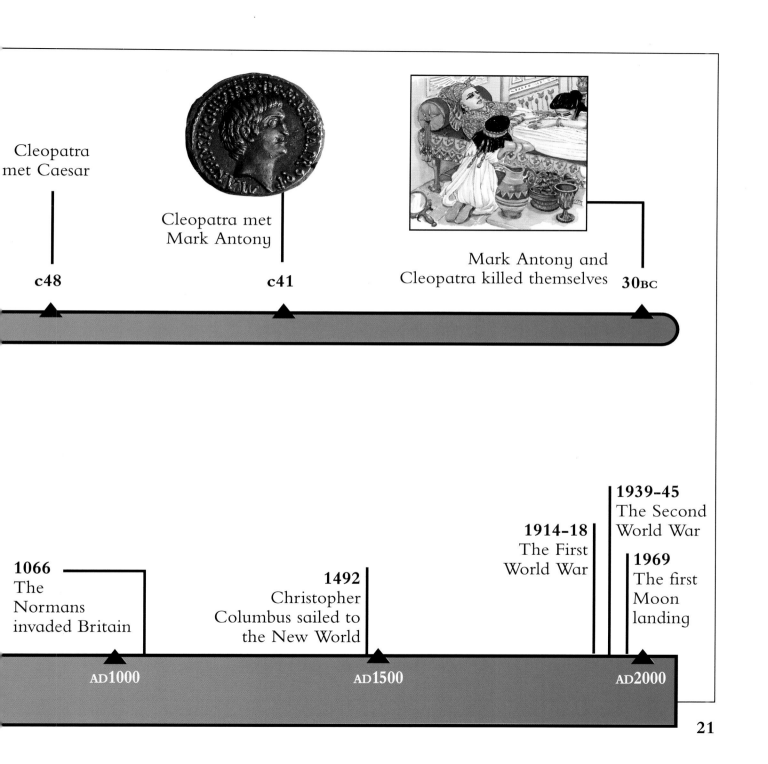

Cleopatra
met Caesar

Cleopatra met
Mark Antony

Mark Antony and
Cleopatra killed themselves

c48

c41

30BC

1066
The
Normans
invaded Britain

1492
Christopher
Columbus sailed to
the New World

1914–18
The First
World War

1939–45
The Second
World War

1969
The first
Moon
landing

AD1000

AD1500

AD2000

How to find out more

More books to read

Cleopatra by Diane Stanler and Peter Vennema (Morrow Junior Books, 1988)

The Egyptians by Rosemary Rees (Heinemann, 1996)

Egypt Photopack by Patricia and Steve Harrison (Folens, 1996)

Egyptian Times by Christopher Maynard (Kingfisher, 1996)

World History by various authors (Classical World, Kingfisher, 1997)

Egyptian Quest by Herbie Brennan (Kingfisher, 1997)

Cleopatra, From History to Legend by Edith Flamarion (New Horizons 1997)

Who was Cleopatra? by Geraldine Harris (MacDonald Young Books/Wayland, 1997)

Eureka! Ancient Egypt by various authors (Channel 4, 1997)

Places to visit or to which to write

British Museum,
Great Russell Street,
London WC1.
Tel 0171 636 1555

History in Evidence,
Monk Road,
Alfreton,
Derbyshire DE55 7RL.
Tel 0800 318686

Liverpool Museum,
William Brown Street,
Liverpool L3 8EN
Tel 0151 478 4399

Manchester Museum
Oxford Road
Manchester M13 9PL
Tel 0161 275 2634

Glossary

ancestor *(4)* Someone in your family tree, such as parents and grandparents.

astronomy *(7)* The study of the stars.

banquet *(17)* A fine dinner with many courses.

capital *(4)* Main city, where the government is.

causeway *(6)* A narrow piece of land which links an island to the mainland.

conquer *(4)* To defeat and take over a country through war.

consul *(14)* In Roman times, one of the two elected rulers of Rome.

exports *(9)* Things sold to other countries.

famine *(9)* A shortage of food when there has not been enough rain for crops to grow.

hieroglyphic *(5)* Egyptian writing which had symbols and pictures.

linen *(9)* Cloth made from fibres of the flax plant.

lyre *(7)* A stringed instrument which was plucked like a guitar.

merchant *(14)* Someone who buys and sells goods.

ochre *(10)* A red or yellow mineral.

papyrus *(9)* A kind of stiff paper made from rushes.

pharaoh *(4)* The ruler of Egypt.

Pharos *(6)* The first known lighthouse.

Senate *(15)* The Assembly (people) which ruled Rome.

siege *(15)* A blockade in which an army surrounds a building or a town.

villa *(15)* A country house.

terracotta *(7)* Reddish-brown pottery.

Index